Historic

California

Its Colorful Names
And How It Got Them

By Alton Pryor

Historic California

Its Colorful Names and How It Got Them

By Alton Pryor

Stagecoach Publishing

5360 Campcreek Loop
Roseville, CA. 95747
(916) 771-8166

Historic

California

Its Colorful Names and Places

Copyright © 2002 by Alton Pryor

ISBN: 0-9660053-8-4

First Edition 2002

Stagecoach Publishing

5360 Campcreek Loop
Roseville, CA. 95747
Phone: (916) 771-8166
stagecoachpublishing@surewest.net

Other books by Alton Pryor:

"Little Known Tales in California History"
"Classic Tales in California History"
"Those Wild and Lusty Gold Camps"
"Outlaws and Gunslingers"
"California's Hidden Gold"
"Jonathan's Red Apple Tree" (Children)

Stagecoach Publishing
5360 Campcreek Loop
Roseville, CA. 95747
Phone: (916) 771-8166
stagecoach publishing@surewest.com

I have fallen in love with American names,
The sharp names that never get fat,
The snakeskin titles of mining claims,
The plumed war bonnet of Medicine Hat,
Tucson and Deadwood and Lost Mule Flat.

Stephen Vincent Benet

Forward

Nothing seems to bring California's rich history alive more than its colorful place names. These names document many of the people who have lived here and had a major influence on their communities.

While the "Gold Rush" towns had wildly colorful names, they were no more so than those of Spanish and European heritage.

Because of the preponderance of names that proliferate the state, it is necessary to confine this book to those that have the most historical interest or at least provide a good story.

We are envious of Father Font, a diarist with Juan Bautista de Anza's expedition, who had the job of arriving at so many of these wonderful names that grace California's towns. That would be a nice job to have.

This book, we feel, fills a need in furthering the knowledge of those who want to know more about the grand state in which they live.

We are sorry if we have left out the name of any reader's favorite California place name. We would also like to hear from readers about possible names that should be considered should we pursue a second printing. The author can be contacted at Stagecoach Publishing, 5360 Campcreek Loop, Roseville, CA. 95747.

Alton Pryor

Acampo (San Joaquin County)

(ah-kahm-poh)   In   Spanish,   the   name   means "common pasture or camp. Acampo is located in the San Joaquin County in Central California. It is an agricultural area with a proud history.

Adelanto (San Bernardino)

Modern application is a Spanish word meaning "advance" or "progress".

Agua Caliente (Hot Springs, Sonoma County)

(ah-gwah cahl-yayn-tay) In Spanish the name means hot water. *Aguas Calientes* means hot waters; Aguas Frias (Butte County) means cold water. The Agua Caliente name was applied to many California creeks and springs and several Spanish land grants.

Ahwahnee—(Yosemite Valley)

(ah-wah-nee) Awani is a Yokuts Indian word, signifying a deep or grassy valley, which was their name for Yosemite Valley. The Yokuts had a large village at the foot of Yosemite Falls.

Alameda—(City, Alameda County)

In Spanish, an *alameda* is an avenue or boulevard shaded by trees. It is derived from Alamo (ah-lah-

8

moh), the Spanish word for poplar or cottonwood. Alameda was first called Encinal (ayn-see-nahl), which means oak grove.

Alamo

(al-a-moh)   The Spanish name for poplar or cottonwood is found in the names of creeks, rivers, mountains, and valleys. There is a town by that name in Contra Costa County.

Albion—(Town in Mendocino County)

(al-bee-on) This is the name given to California by Sir Francis Drake. New Albion is an ancient name for Britain. Cartographers designated California as "Nueva (New) Albion on early maps.

Alcatraz (Island in San Francisco Bay)

(ahl-cah-trahs) Taken from the Spanish "La Isla de los Alcatraces" (The Island of the Pelicans). Juan Manuel de Ayala, the first navigator to sail into San Francisco Bay, gave the name to nearby Yerba Buena Island where many of these birds were seen. A mapmaker later transferred the name to the little island, often called "The Rock". A federal penitentiary was once located there. It is now a state park.

Alhambra (Los Angeles County)

This tract was opened in 1874 and was named for the Moorish Palace in Spain. Alhambra Valley in Contra

Costa County is a euphonious rendering of the Spanish name *Canada del Hambre* (valley of hunger).

Alisal (Monterey County)

(ahl-e-sahl) Taken from the Spanish word, aliso, "alder tree", meaning a grove of alders, or sometimes sycamores. Alisal occupies one of two original land grants and was the site of the first secular college in California, founded on Alisal Creek in 1834 by William E.P. Harnell.

Aliso

The Spanish name for alder tree was often used for place names in Spanish times and has survived in some areas of the state.

Almaden (Santa Clara County)

A quicksilver mine there was developed in 1846. It was named after the famous mines in Spain. The post office is now again New Almaden. New Almaden was the site of the first mining in California. The Ohlone Indians dug for cinnabar there to use as the base for their red paint.

Alpine (San Diego County)

The town began as a stage stop for the mines in the Cuyamaca Mountains. Drivers hauling supplies to the mines and delivering gold to San Diego stopped to rest and change horses. It's name came from its obvious scenic beauty and fresh water. A U.S. Government survey during World War 1 declared Alpine's climate the most equable in the nation.

Alturas (Modoc County)

A branch of Pit River or Achomawe Tribe of Native Americans originally occupied what is now Alturas before white men arrived in the area. The village was known as Kosealekte. The valley is a prehistoric lakebed, which formed from alternating erosion and rebuilding of the volcanic flows of the Modoc Plateau. In 1876 the residents petition the legislature to change the name from Dorrisville to the present Spanish name meaning 'heights'.

Alum Rock (Both an avenue and a residential district in San Jose, Santa Clara County.)

It is named for California's oldest park, Alum Rock Park, in Alum Rock Canyon. It was named for a 200-foot high alum-bearing rock near its entrance. It is on public lands confirmed to San Jose by the King of Spain in 1779 and was made a public park by an act of the California Legislature in 1872.

Alvarado (Alameda County)

Named in 1853 for Juan Bautista Alvarado, governor of California 1836-1842).

Alviso (Santa Clara County)

Founded in 1849 and named for Ignacio Alviso, who came as a child with the Anza expedition in 1776 and settled here in 1838.

Amador (County in Mother Lode)

Named after Amador Creek, which in turn was named after Jose Maria Amador, a soldier from the San Francisco presidio. In 1848, Amador and a group of Indians established a mining camp near the present town of Amador City.

Amargosa River (Death Valley)

Fremont recorded it in April 1844. Spaniards called the stream *Amargosa,* bitter water of the desert."

Amboy (San Bernardino County)

Railroad stations from here to the Arizona line (1883) were originally in alphabetical order after eastern stations (Amboy, Bristol, Cadiz, Danby, Edson, Fenner, Goffs.)

American River

The name originates from *El Paso de los Americanos.* Spanish speaking Indians called the Canadian trappers traversing the river "Americanos". John Sutter frequently used the name.

Anacapa Island (Ventura County)

The name is a Chumash Indian word, which has been listed with various spellings. The present spelling is found on Spanish maps. Of the eight Channel Islands, Anacapa is the only one with a name of non-Hispanic origin.

Anaheim (Orange County)

Settled by Germans in 1858, this colony was named after the river Santa Ana, plus the suffix, *"heim"*, meaning home.

Angel Island (San Francisco Bay)

While commanding the *"San Carlos"*, which anchored in San Francisco Bay in 1775, Juan Manuel de Ayala named the island "La Isla de Nuestra Senora de Los Angeles" (The Island of Our Lady of the Angels). It is now a state park.

Angels Camp (City in Calaveras County)

Named for George Angel, a member of Colonel Jonathan D. Stevenson's regiment of First New York Volunteers. Angel established the trading post, which was named after him.

Antioch (City, Contra Costa County)

Smith's Landing, as it was originally called, was named for the first settlers, the twin brothers Joseph H. and W.W. Smith, who were farmers and ordained ministers. They arrived in 1849 from Boston and induced other New Englanders to settle the area in 1850. In 1852, at a Fourth of July picnic, residents decided to rename the community Antioch, after the biblical city in Syria.

Aptos (Town, Santa Cruz County)

(ap-tahs) Aptos was named by the American Indians who lived there for thousands of years before the Spanish completed Mission Santa Cruz in 1794. In 1833 the government of Mexico granted Aptos Rancho to Rafael Castro.

Arcadia (Los Angeles County)

It was named in 1888 after the district in Greece, symbolized in poetry as a place of rural simplicity.

Arroyo

(a-roi-oh) California has more than 150 streams and gulches that include in their names the word Arroyo, which means "watercourse".

Artois (Glenn County)

Called Germantown in 1876, the place was given this French name in 1918.

Asilomar (Monterey County)

(a-see-lo-mar) An artificial name coined by the National Board of the YWCA in 1913. The name uses the Spanish word *asilo* (refuge) and *mar* (sea).

Atascadero (San Luis Obispo County)

(a-tas-ka-dehr-oh) a pleasant sounding name, but in actuality it means mud hole, or miry place.

Auburn (City, Placer County)

One of California's earliest gold mining camps, Auburn was known by several names between the spring of 1848 and the fall of 1849. Among them were: Wood's Dry Diggings, North Fork Dry Diggings, and Rich Dry Diggings. Eventually, it was named for a settler's home in Auburn, New York.

Azusa (City, Los Angeles County)

Azusa is an Indian name, derived from that of a nearby hill, which the Indians called "Azuncsabit, meaning, "skunk hill or place."

Balboa (Orange County)

(bahl-boh-ah) Vasco Nunez de Balboa, Castilian nobleman, discovered the Pacific Ocean at Darien, Panama in 1513.

Bakersfield (Kern County)

A few families who trekked northward through El Tejon Pass, seeking home sites rather than gold, settled Bakersfield in 1858. Colonel Thomas Baker invited weary travelers and teamsters to park their wagons and rest in an area that became known as "Colonel Baker's field.

Baldwin Park (Los Angeles County)

Named after E.J. "Lucky" Baldwin, a spectacular financier in the 1890s, who built Santa Anita Racetrack. The town was built on his former estate. Baldwin Lake (San Bernardino County) was named for him.

Banning (Riverside County)

The town was named in 1885 for Phineas Banning of Delaware. He was one of the outstanding pioneers in the development of the Los Angeles District.

Barstow (San Bernardino County)

Named in 1866 by the Santa Fe R.R. for its president, William Barstow Strong.

Beckwourth (Pass, Lassen and Plumas counties; Town, Plumas County.

Both Beckwourth Pass and the town of Beckwourth were named for James Beckwourth, the son of a black slave woman and a white Revolutionary War army officer. He discovered the emigrant pass bearing his name, and which considerably shortened the travel for wagon trains coming to California.

Benicia (City, Solano County)

(bay-nee-syah) Named in honor of Francisca Benicia, wife of General Mariano G. Vallejo. It was California's state capitol for 13 months in 1853 and 1854.

Berkeley (City, Alameda County)

A member of the committee assigned to select a site for the University of California, on viewing San Francisco Bay and the Golden Gate, quoted a stanza by George Berkeley, Bishop of Cloyne, beginning: "Westward the course of empire takes its way." A confrere said, "Why not name it Berkeley."

Big Pine (Inyo County)

The "big pine" for which the town was named has disappeared. Now a lone, yet majestic, sequoia stands near the spot where the big pine once stood. Remnants of former irrigation canals can be seen. The Los Angeles

Municipal Water Department purchased riparian water rights, and drained the area of its water supply.

Bishop (Inyo County)

Samuel A. Bishop, for whom the town was named, was a well-known cattleman who came to California in 1849.

Blythe (Riverside County)

The town was named for Thomas H. Blythe, a San Francisco promoter of irrigation in the 1870's.

Bodega (Bay, Town, Sonoma County)

(boh-day-gah) The name honors the discoverer of the bay, Juan Francisco de la Bodega y Quadra.

Borego (San Diego County)

Borego is the Spanish word for sheep or lamb and was frequently used for place names during Spanish times.

Brawley (Imperial County)

The town was named for J.H. Braly, of Los Angeles. When Braly objected to the use of his name, because he didn't feel the community had a good future, the present name was substituted. The town is now a thriving community and the second largest shipping area for produce in California.

Brea (Orange County)

Brea refers to pitch, tar, or asphalt beds. The town got its name from Rancho La Brea. In Los Angeles County the word *brea* is used to name the La Brea tar pits where the bones of many prehistoric animals, including the saber-toothed cat and the ground sloth, have been recovered.

Burlingame (San Mateo County)

Named by William C. Ralston, an early San Francisco financier, for his friend, Anson Burlingame, U.S. minister to China (1861-1867).

Butte (County)

One of California's original 27 counties, it was named for the Sutter or Marysville Buttes, both of which were originally in Butte County. Because of later changes in the county boundary, the Buttes are now across the line in Sutter County.

Cabazon (Riverside County)

The station was named in the 1870's, after a rancheria near by, which was so named because the chief had an unusually large head (*cabezon*).

Cabrillo (Explorer)

(cah-bree-yoh) Juan Rodriguez Cabrillo, Portuguese navigator, sailing under the flag of Spain, discovered San Diego Bay in 1542.

Cache Creek (Yolo County)

The Hudson Bay trappers, who cached their furs and supplies in the area, named it Cache Creek.

Cahuenga Pass (Los Angeles County)

(ka-wenga-ga or ka-hung-ga) The pass derived its name from the Cahuengo Rancho, which was named after an Indian rancheria mentioned as *Caguenga* as early as 1802. At "Campo de Cahuenga" General Andres Pico surrendered to Fremont, January 13, 1847.

Cajon Pass (San Bernardino County)

(ka-hohn) The name means "box" in Spanish, and was used to describe the "boxlike" canyons.

Calaveras (Calaveras County)

(kal-a-vehr-as) The name means "skulls", and was so-called because a number of human skulls were found littering the ground, signifying either a fight or a famine. The name is also applied to the Calaveras River.

Calistoga (Napa County)

Samuel Brannan, its founder, envisioned the place as the Saratoga of the West, and drew on "California" and "Saratoga" to form the name.

Cambria (San Luis Obispo County)

Settled in the 1860's and given the Roman name of ancient Wales.

Camino

(ka-mee-noh) The name is the Spanish word for "road". El Camino Real (the public highway) connected the string of California missions along the coast. It is often erroneously interpreted to mean "the king's highway."

Carmel-by-the-Sea (Monterey County)

Its name was derived from the Rio de Carmelo (Carmel River), which was named by Vizcaino in 1602 after the Carmelite Order who were members of his expedition.

Carpenteria (Santa Barbara County)

(kar-pin-te-ree-a) Soldiers named this village La Carpenteria (carpenter shop) after seeing native Indians building a canoe on shore.

Carquinez (Strait, Upper San Francisco Bay)

(cahr-kee-nez) The name is derived from the Karquin Indians.

Carrizo Creek (San Diego, Imperial counties)

(kah-ree-soh) The presence of carrizo (reed grass) prompted the name to the stream, and was mentioned by Father Font, a diarist, when the Anza party camped here December 13, 1775.

Casmalia (Santa Barbara County)

This is believed to be a Spanish rendering of an Indian word. The meaning of the word is no longer known.

Castaic (Los Angeles and Kern Counties)

(kas-tayk) It is believed the Chumash Indians called the village at the foot of the trail *Kashtik* (my eyes or our eye), but the name now is used in the sense of view. The name of the lake and the valley in Kern County was spelled Castac.

Cayucos (San Luis Obispo)

(kah-yoo-kas) The word appears as part of a land grant of 1857 and 1842, *Morro y Cayucos*. The name is derived from *cayuco* (fishing canoe), which may be a Spanish rendering of the Eskimo kayak.

Cazadero (Sonoma County)

(kaz-a-deh-roh) The name means hunting place in Spanish. The name was also applied to the terminal of the North Pacific Coast Railroad in the late 1880's.

Ceres (Stanislaus County)

The name of the Roman goddess of growing vegetation was given to the station shortly after this part of the Central Pacific Railroad was built in 1870-1871.

Cerrito

The word means "small hill", and has been a favorite geographical term in Spanish California.

Chico (Butte County)

(chee-coh) Meaning little, the word is derived from *Rancho del Arroyo Chico* (Ranch of the Little Creek), purchased by General John Bidwell.

Chino (San Bernardino County)

In Mexico and other Spanish-speaking countries, the term designates a person of mixed blood. The chief of the original village on the *Santa Ana del Chino* grant was probably a chino.

Cholame (San Luis Obispo County)

(sho-lam) The name of a Salinan Indian rancheria, mentioned as Cholan in 1803, and applied to the Cholam land grant in 1844.

Chowchilla (Madera, Mariposa counties)

The *Chauciles* Indians are mentioned repeatedly in the 1850's as horse thieves. The name was applied to the river in the 1850's.

Chula Vista (San Diego County)

Derived from the Mexican word *"chula"*, meaning pretty or graceful, and with the Spanish word for "view".

Cienega

(see-en-ega) The Spanish word for marsh, it is often used to designate a meadow in America.

Coachella (Riverside County)

The valley north of the Salton Sea was named for the Cahuilla Indians. The name Coachella Valley was originally suggested when the area was surveyed before 1900, but was discarded. The word Coachella, itself, is apparently meaningless.

Coalinga (Fresno County)

(koh-ling-ga) It was originally called Coaling Station in 1888, when a Southern Pacific official created a new name by adding an a to "coaling".

Colfax (Placer County)

The Central Pacific named this community in 1865 for Schuyler Colfax, who at that time was Speaker of the House, and later vice president to Ulysses Grant.

Coloma (El Dorado County)

This is the site where James Marshall discovered gold in 1848. The town, which developed around Sutter's Mill where gold was discovered, was named after a Maidu Indian village.

Colusa (County Seat for Colusa County)

The name is a corruption of Ko-ru-si (also spelled Co-lu-si and Co-lu-se. The name is said to mean "scratcher", because it was the privilege of tribal brides to begin the honeymoon by scratching the faces of their braves. One source says Colusa derives from the name of a rancheria, *Coru,* mentioned in documents dating back to 1821.

Concord (Contra Costa County)

This settlement was first named *Todos Santos* (All Saints) in 1862 by its founder, Salvio Pacheco, who was owner of Rancho del Diablo. The name was later changed to Concord after the historic town in Massachusetts.

Conejo (Ventura County)

(ko-nay-o) This is the Spanish name for rabbit, and it is found repeatedly in place names of Spanish California. It was also applied to a land grant in 1822.

Contra Costa (Name of County)

Meaning opposite coast, the name was originally applied to the entire shore of San Francisco opposite the Peninsula. The County was created and named in 1850.

Converse (Fresno County)

This town was named for Charles Converse, who acquired timberlands in the valley in the 1870's. He built the first jail in the county and was the first to be confined in it.

Corona (Riverside County)

The name is the Latin word for circle, and the community was so-named because of the circular drive around the city.

Coronado (San Diego County)

(Coh-roh-nah-doh) It is named for the islands off the coast of Lower California, *Los Coronados*, and not for explorer Francisco Vasquez de Coronado. Vizcaino named these islands in 1602.

Corte Madera (Marin County)

The origin of the name, which means, "place where lumber or timber is cut," is found in the *Corte de Madera del Presidio* land grant of 1834.

Costa Mesa (Orange County)

The name is an Americanized combination of two Spanish words, *costa* (coast) and *mesa* (tableland). The name was chosen as the result of a contest.

Cosumnes River (Sacramento County)

(ko-sum-nes) The name stems from Miwok Indian words *Kosum* (salmon) and *umne* (tribe). John Sutter used the present spelling in 1841. It was also used in two land grants of 1844.

Cotati (Sonoma County)

The name of an Indian rancheria, *kotati*, was applied in the present form to a land grant in 1844.

Covelo (Mendocino County)

(koh-ve-loh) While some believe it was named after a fortress in Switzerland, it is more likely named after *Covolo*, the old Venetian fort in adjoining Tirol.

Coyote

(ky-oh-tee) This is a western American adaptation of the Mexican name for the prairie wolf (*coyotl*) and an extremely popular place name in California. In the mining districts, the term "coyoteing) referred to irregular shafts or burrows, comparing them to the holes of coyotes.

Crescent City (Del Norte)

It was named in the 1850's for its crescent-shaped bay.

Cucamonga (San Bernardino)

A Shoshonean Indian place name, it means "sandy place". It was first mentioned in 1819 and transferred to a land grant in 1839.

Cuesta Pass (San Luis Obispo County)

(kwest-a) This Spanish name for "grade" was applied to a station north of the pass when Southern Pacific Railroad engineers achieved the difficult crossing of the Santa Lucia Range, 1877-1894.

Cupertino (Santa Clara County)

(kew-per-tee-no) Named by Spanish explorers for the nearby *Arroyo de San Jose Cupertino* in honor of a seventeenth century Italian saint. The arroyo is now Stevens Creek, but the post office preserves the old name.

Cuyama River (Ventura, San Luis Obispo, Santa Barbara counties)

Derived from a Chumash Indian place name, *Kuyam*, meaning clams. The present spelling is repeatedly found in land grants.

Death Valley

The Indians called the valley *Tomesha* (ground afire). A large part of the valley is below sea level. A party of gold rush emigrants who had suffered extreme hardship in crossing the valley applied the English name to the valley. As they left the area after days of exhaustion, they took off their hats and said, "Goodbye, Death Valley."

Del Monte (Monterey County)

The name, meaning, "of the grove", was applied to the Del Monte hotel in 1886. The grove reference was probably suggested by the beautiful oak groves in the area.

Del Norte (County)

The Spanish phrase "of the north" was bestowed on this new county by the legislature in 1857.

Descanso (San Diego County)

In Spanish, the name means "repose". The name was applied to the post office in the 1880's.

Diablo (A mountain in Contra Costa County)

The name means "Devil" in Spanish, and the mountain, *Monte del Diablo*, means "Mountain of the Devil". One legend, as told by Gen. Mariano Guadalupe Vallejo, is that an Indian tribe of Bolgones, fighting Spanish soldiers from San Francisco, had a medicine man called Puy or Pui (Evil Spirit) who appeared from the mountain caves to inspire them to victory.

Donner (Lake, Pass, and Peak in Nevada and Placer Counties)

Named for the tragic Donner party, headed by George and Jacob Donner and James F. Reed, which was marooned in the deep snow near the lake in the winter of 1846-1847. Forty-two in the party lost their lives due to cold and starvation. Some in the party resorted to cannibalism.

Don Pedro Reservoir (Tuolumne County)

The reservoir was named after Don Pedro's Bar, a mining site, which in turn was named for Pierre (Don Pedro) Sainsevain, a French pioneer of 1839 who mined the bar in 1849.

Dos Palos (Merced County)

Named by the Southern Pacific Railroad in 1889. The name, in Spanish, means "two trees".

Dos Rios (Mendocino County)

Name means "two rivers" and was so named because of the town's location at the junction of two branches of the Eel River.

Downey (Los Angeles County)

Named in 1865 for John G. Downey, governor of California from 1860 to 1862. He subdivided his Santa Gertrudis Rancho and gave his name to the new town.

Downieville (Sierra County)

Named for William Downie, a Scot who mined gold at the forks of the Yuba River in 1849.

Ducor (Tulare County)

Southern Pacific's station was once called Dutch Corners. It was given the abbreviated version of the former name, "Dutch Corners", where the homesteads of four German settlers joined.

Dunsmuir (Siskiyou County)

The name was applied to the railroad station in 1886 for Alexander Dunsmuir, coal baron of British Columbia and San Francisco. Dunsmuir donated a fountain to the station to show his appreciation.

Earlimart (Tulare County)

An advertising slogan applied in 1909 to indicate that crops mature early in the area. The town, once known as "Alila", was also the site of an early-day train-robbery attempt by the famous Dalton Brothers outlaw gang.

Ebbetts Pass (Alpine County)

It was named in 1854 for John Ebbetts, who had crossed the pass with a mule train in April 1851.

Edwards (Kern County)

This is the site of Edwards Air Force Base. The town was named in 1950 in honor of Captain Glenn W. Edwards, who was killed in an experimental flight.

Eel River (Mendocino and Humboldt Counties)

The Gregg exploring party in January 1850 named the river. The party had obtained large quantities of eels from the Indians in exchange for a broken frying pan.

El Cajon (San Diego County)

(Ka-hohn) The name, in Spanish, means box, such as canyons boxed in by hills or cliffs. Historians mention El Cajon as early 1821 as the name of a rancho held by Mission San Diego.

El Capitan (Yosemite National Park)

The Mariposa Battalion named this giant rock in 1851 when they discovered the valley. The party assumed that El Capitan (the captain, or chief) was the Spanish translation of the Indian name for the rock.

El Centro (Imperial County)

The town's Spanish name was applied because the community was located near the center of the Imperial Valley.

El Cerrito (Contra Costa County)

(ser-ree-toh) This town's Spanish name means little hill, named for the isolated knoll at the bay shore. In

1850, it was recorded as *Serrito de San Antonio,* and later as *Cerrito de San Pablo.*

El Dorado (El Dorado County and town)

The name, meaning "the gilded one" was used at the beginning of the sixteenth century for a mythical Indian chief who would cover himself with gold dust for the performance of ceremonies.

El Monte (Los Angeles County)

This town was settled in the 1850's. It was called *Monte*, which, in Spanish, means grove or thicket. It was supposedly named for the dense growth of willows in the area.

El Portal (Yosemite Valley)

In Spanish, it means "the gate". It stands at the entrance of Yosemite Valley.

El Segundo (Los Angeles County)

Standard Oil Company named this community in 1911. The name signifies that this is the site of the company's second refinery in California.

Elsinore (Riverside County)

Named in 1884 after the Danish castle made famous by Shakespeare's Hamlet.

Embarcadero

This Spanish word means, "landing place." The name is used in a number of communities throughout the state.

Emerson, Mount (Inyo County)

John Muir named this peak for Ralph Waldo Emerson, the American poet and philosopher. Emerson visited Yosemite in 1871.

Emeryville (Alameda County)

This town was named for Joseph Emery, who, in 1859, bought the land on which the town now sits.

Encanto (San Diego)

In Spanish, the name means "enchantment". The name was used by the post office here in the 1890's.

Encinitas (San Diego County)

(en-si-nee-tas) The area was settled in the 1880's and was named after *Canada de los Encinitos* (valley of the little oaks). Encina (live oak) and its diminative, *encinita,* is frequent in California place names.

Escalon (San Joaquin County)

(Ays-cah-lohn) The name, in Spanish, means step or stepping stone.

Escondido (San Diego County)

(es-kon-dee-doh) The name is the Spanish word for "hidden". It was applied to the subdivision in 1885. There are four Escondido Creeks in southern counties.

Espada Creek (San Diego County)

On August 27, 1769, an Indian from a nearby village stole the sword of one of Portola's soldiers. The town was then named *Rancheria de la Espada* (village of the sword).

Estero

(es-the-roh) The Spanish word for inlet or estuary is frequently used along the ocean shore.

Estrella (San Luis Obispo County)

The name means "stars" in Spanish. It was applied to the community because four valleys diverge like the rays of a star at the original site of the ranch.

Etiwanda (San Bernardino County)

Named in the early 1880's for the chief of an Indian tribe near Lake Michigan.

Ettersburg (Humboldt County)

The post office was named in 1904 for Albert F. Etter, creator of new fruit varieties.

Eureka (Humboldt County)

This may be the oldest city in the United States bearing this name, which is a Greek expression meaning "I have found it." The word was adopted in 1849 as the motto for the Great Seal of the State of California.

Exeter (Tulare County)

Settled by English settlers, they chose to name it after the city in England of the same name.

Fairfax (Marin County)

The city was named after Charles ("Lord") Fairfax of Fairfax County, Virginia, who settled in the area in 1856.

Fairfield (Solano County)

Robert Waterman, a clipper-ship captain, named the city after his former home in Connecticut.

Fall River (Shasta County)

Named by John C. Fremont in 1846 because of its falls and cascades.

Fandango (Modoc County)

While undocumented, it is said that an immigrant party gave the name to the valley in 1849. One source says it was so cold one night that the immigrants were forced to dance all night in order to keep warm.

Farallon Islands (San Francisco County)

This is the Spanish name for small rocky islands in the sea, and is shown on old maps of the coast. The rocks outside Golden Gate were mentioned as *farallones* by the Vizcaino expedition in 1603, and were named *Farallones de los Frayles* by Bodega in 1775.

Feather River

Named *Rio de las Plumas* (river of feathers) in the 1840's because of the many feathers worn by the Indians and the feathers scattered over the landscape. Hudson's Bay trappers had used the name, "Feather River," in the 1830's, but it was upon Sutter's statement that the name was put on the maps.

Felton (Santa Cruz County)

The town was named in 1878 for Charles N. Felton, congressman, 1885-1889 and U.S. senator (1891-1893).

Fiddletown (Amador County)

First called "Fiddletown" during the early days of the gold rush. Most of the miners who settled the area were from Missouri and many of them possessed and played fiddles. The name was changed, in 1876 to Oleta because Judge Purinton didn't like being referred to as "the man from Fiddletown" when he traveled to San Francisco and Sacramento.

Fillmore (Ventura County)

Town was named in 1887 for J.A. Fillmore, general superintendent of the Southern Pacific Railroad. Fillmore is located in the Santa Clara River Valley, just north of the river along Highway 126.

Firebaugh (Fresno County)

In 1854, A.D. Fierbaugh established a trading post and ferry at this point. The name was misspelled when it was used as a stage station in the 1860's.

Flintridge (Los Angeles County)

Named in 1920 for Frank P. Flint, U.S. Senator, 1905-1911.

Folsom (Sacramento County)

Laid out by railroad engineer Theodore Judah in 1855, Folsom was intended to be the terminus of the Sacramento Valley Railroad, the first rail line in California. The town is named for Joseph L. Folsom, assistant quartermaster of the New York Volunteers in 1847. He was owner of the rancho on which the town now sits.

Fontana (San Bernardino County)

While the town was named in 1913 for the Fontana Development Company, the name may be the Spanish poetical word for fountain, or the name of a family. It was selected as the site of a steel mill in 1942.

Fort Bragg (Mendocino County)

A military post was established in 1857 and named for Colonel Braxton Bragg, Mexican War veteran and afterward confederates general.

Fort Jones (Siskiyou County)

In 1860's, settlers named the town after the fort in gratitude for the military protection they had received. The fort was named for Colonel Roger Jones, adjutant general of the army.

Fort Ross (Sonoma County)

This was a Russian settlement established on September 11, 1812. Until the Russians arrived, San Francisco was the northern limit of Spanish settlement. Ross is an obsolete, poetical name for "Russians".

Fortuna (Humboldt County)

Originally called "Fortune" in the 1870's, the name was changed to its present form because residents felt it sounded better and still had the same advertising value.

Fourth Crossing (Calaveras County)

The rich placers of San Antonio Creek were first located in 1848. Shortly afterwards, David Foreman settled in the area and established a combination trading post, saloon and hotel for which the site was early known as Foremans Ranch. The place soon came to be called Fourth Crossing; however, as it was located at the fourth river crossing on the road between Stockton and Angels Camp.

Fremont (Alameda County)

Named in honor of John C. Fremont (1813-1890), who one of the most famous and popular of explorers. Fremont grew up as the illegitimate child of a prominent woman of Virginia society, and a penniless French refugee. The circumstances of his birth made the young Fremont an ambitious man, a social climber. Throughout his career he would seek out the patronage of powerful men,

Fresno (Fresno County)

The name is Spanish for "ash". It was applied because the tree is native to the area. The "German Syndicate" of which Frederick Roeding was a leader, founded the town in 1868. The County of Fresno was created in 1856.

Friant (Fresno County)

The town was originally called "Converse Ferry". Later, it was called Pollasky. In the early 1920's, the name was changed to honor Thomas Friant, who, with T.S. White, father of Stewart Edward White, a western screenwriter, formed the White and Friant Lumber Company.

Fullerton (Orange County)

Named for G.H. Fullerton in 1887. He was president of a development company that established the town.

Funeral Mountains (Death Valley)

Light-colored rock formations capped with heavy masses of black limestone give the mountains the appearance of being fringed with crepe.

Gabilan Range (Monterey and San Benito Counties)

Gabilan Peak was named for the sparrow hawk, which in Spanish is pronounced *gavilan* or *gabilan*. Known by this name since 1828, it is often called Fremont Peak.

Gallinas (Marin County)

A *sitio de las Gallenas* (place of the hens) was mentioned in 1817.

Garberville (Humboldt County)

The post office was named for Jacob C. Garber, the first settler in the area, in 1844.

Garcia River (Mendocino)

This river was named for Rafael Garcia, who had a land grant here in 1844. The Garcia River in Mendocino County is one of California's best-loved wild steelhead fisheries.

Gardena (Los Angeles County)

The name, obviously coined from "garden", was applied to the subdivision in the 1880's.

Gardener, Mount (Fresno County)

Named for James T. Gardiner in 1865. He was a member of the Whitney Survey.

Gaviota (Santa Barbara County)

(gah-vee-oh-tah) In Spanish, it is the word for "sea gull". It was so-named because a soldier in the Portola expedition killed a sea gull there on August 17, 1769.

Gazelle (Siskiyou County)

The name was given to the post office in 1874. It may have been named after the African antelope to distinguish it from the native antelope.

Gerber (Tehama County)

The post office and railroad station were given the name in 1916 in honor of H.E. Gerber of Sacramento.

Gibbs, Mount (Yosemite National Park)

It was named for Oliver W. Gibbs in 1864. He was a professor of science at Harvard.

Gilroy (Santa Clara County)

The city was named for John Gilroy, a Scotch sailor, who arrived in California in 1814. He settled in the

Santa Clara Valley and came into possession of the land on which the city is situated in 1833.

Glendale (Los Angeles County)

Founded on the Rancho San Rafael about 1880, it was first named Riverdale. When the post office was established, the name was changed because there was a Riverdale post office located in Fresno County.

Glendora (Los Angeles County)

George Whitcomb named the city in 1887, coining the word by combining "glen" with his wife's name, "Ledora".

Glenn County

Formed in 1891, the county was named for Dr. Hugh J. Glenn, pioneer of 1849, and for many years, the leading wheat grower in California.

Goddard, Mount (Kings Canyon National Park)

The Whitney Survey named the mountain for George H. Goddard, a native of England, and a leading civil engineer in California.

Goethe, Mount (Fresno County)

The highest peak of the Glacier Divide, it was named in 1949, the bicentennial year of the birth of Johann Wolfgang Goethe, poet and philosopher.

Golden Gate

Named by John C. Fremont in 1846. He chose the name because he envisioned the day when riches of the Orient would flow through the gate. He had not, however, anticipated the discovery of gold in California, which might have added new significance to the name.

Goleta (Santa Barbara County)

(go-lee-ta) The Spanish word for "schooner", it was used as a name for a land grant in 1846. It is not known whether the name was applied because of a wreck of schooner in the estuary or because a vessel was built there in 1829.

Gonzales (Monterey County)

Name given to the railroad station in 1873 for Teodoro Gonzales because it was built on his extensive land grant.

Graciosa (Santa Barbara County)

Soldiers in Portola's expedition applied the name, which, in Spanish, means, "the graceful one" on August 31, 1769.

Grass Valley (Nevada County)

The post office, which was established in 1850, was originally called Centerville. Soon after, it was changed to its present-day descriptive name, which at the time was a name as unique in the United States as Centerville was common. Immigrants had named the spot "Grassy Valley" because it provided plenty of forage for their half-starved animals.

Greenfield (Monterey County)

Laid out on the Arroyo Seco Rancho in 1902-1905, the town was at first named for John S. Clarke, of the California Home Extension Association. But the post office objected and the present name was selected from a number of names submitted by residents. It now calls itself the "broccoli capital of the world."

Gridley (Butte County)

It was a Southern Pacific railroad station named in 1870 for George W. Gridley, owner of the land on which it is built.

Griffith Park (Los Angeles County)

The Los Angeles City Council, in 1896, named the park for Griffith J. Griffith, donor of the park area.

Groveland (Tuolumne County)

It was originally called First Garrote (first execution, i.e. hanging), but the name was changed to a more pleasant sound in the 1850's.

Guadalupe (Santa Barbara and San Mateo Counties)

This is a frequently occurring place name in Hispanic countries. The original shrine to Our Lady of Guadalupe was in Spain, but was transferred to Mexico in the 16th century after an Indian had a vision of the Virgin in a town that was renamed Guadalupe. There is a town by this name in Santa Barbara County and in San Mateo County. A river in Santa Clara County was given this name by the Anza expedition in 1776.

Gualala (Sonoma County)

(gwah-la-lah) A Spanish rendering of an Indian phrase, "Where the Waters Meet." There are some historians that attribute the name to a Spanish phonetic application of "Walhalla", which in Teutonic mythology was the abode of heroes fallen in battle.

Guatay (San Diego County)

(gwah-tye) The name is derived from the Diegueno Indian word *kwatai,* meaning large.

Guerneville (Sonoma County)

It was named for George Guerne who built a sawmill at the site in 1864.

Guinda (Yolo County)

(Gween-dah) Means cherry, or wild cherry.

Gustine (Merced County)

It was named for Augustine, the daughter of Henry Miller, a partner in Miller and Lux, California cattle barons.

Hackamore (Modoc County)

The name is a corruption of the Spanish *jaquima,* which is a type of halter used to control horses during the breaking process. The station was called "Jaquima" in 1910, and the spelling changed in 1928.

Haiwee (Inyo County)

The name is taken from an Indian name for dove, *haiwai,* and was recorded as a place name in 1861.

Hamilton, Mount (Santa Clara County)

The town was named for the Rev. Laurentine Hamilton, who climbed to the mountain's top in 1861 with Brewer and Hoffmann of the Whitney Survey.

Hanaupah (Death Valley)

It is believed the name comes from a Panamint Indian word, *"honopi"*, which means "canyon".

Hanford (Kings County)

It was a railroad station, and named, in 1877, for James Hanford, treasurer of Central Pacific Railroad.

Hangtown Creek (Placerville County)

The town of Placerville was once called "Hangtown", because of its propensity to hang its bad men. The name of this creek preserves that nickname.

Harbin Hot Springs (Lake County)

Some think the naturally hot water coming from the hot springs have a healing power. The town was named for James M. Harbin, an immigrant in 1846, who settled at the springs in 1857.

Havasu Lake (San Bernardino County)

This community developed around a man-made lake. The developers named the town for a Mojave Indian word meaning "blue" in 1939. The London Bridge was transported, piece-by-piece, from London to the site, and is now one of the major attractions for visitors.

Havilah (Kern County)

Community was named in 1864 after the Biblical gold land mentioned in Genesis 2:2.

Hawthorne (Los Angeles County)

The town was named for American poet and novelist Nathaniel Hawthorne around 1906.

Hayward (Alameda County)

When Guillermo Castro, grantee of *Rancho San Lorenzo*, laid out the town in 1854, he named it for his friend, William Hayward, who had opened the town's hotel there.

Healdsburg (Sonoma County)

The post office was named in 1857 for Harmon G. Heald, a pioneer in 1846.

Hecker Pass (Santa Clara County)

Named for Henry Hecker, the man who was instrumental in building a highway across the pass.

Hedionda Creek (Santa Clara County)

The name is from the Spanish word for *"fetid"* or *"stinking"*. The name was often applied to malodorous creeks.

Hemet (Riverside County)

Members of the Cahuilla Indian Tribe first inhabited the area. In the early 1800's, it became a cattle ranch for Mission San Luis Rey and was called Rancho San Jacinto. It is the site of the annual Romona Pageant based on a novel by Helen Hunt Jackson.

Hermosa Beach (Los Angeles County)

The name is a Spanish adjective for the word "beautiful". It was applied to the town in 1901.

Hetch Hetchy (Valley, town and reservoir in Tuolumne County.

The name is from Hatchatchie, a Central Miwok Indian name for a grass or plant which grows in the meadow at the lower end of this deep valley, producing edible seeds which the Indians pounded into meal in mortars. The Hetch Hetchy water project is part of San Francisco water supply system.

Hilgard, Mount (Fresno County)

The mountain was named for Professor E.W. Hilgard in 1910. Hilgard was a pioneer of scientific agriculture in California.

Hillsborough (San Mateo County)

The city was incorporated in 1910. The owner of the property named it after Hillsboro, New Hampshire.

Hobart Mills (Nevada County)

It was named in 1897 for Walter Scott Hobart who was a pioneer lumberman in the area.

Hollister (San Benito County)

Named in 1868 for Colonel W.W. Hollister, owner of *San Justo Rancho*, the site on which the town was established. When the name San Justo was first suggested, there was a protest. "There are enough towns named after Saints. It's time we name one after a sinner," said one city father.

Hollywood (Los Angeles County)

It was named in 1886, either after one of the Hollywood's in the east, or very likely after the toyon tree, which is more popularly known as California holly.

Homer's Nose (Sequoia National Park)

It was jokingly named in 1872 after Joseph Homer, one of the members of the surveying party, because others in the party said it looked like Homer's nose.

Honcut (Butte County)

This is a Maidu Indian village name. It was first applied to a land grant in 1844, and to the post office in the 1880's.

Honey Lake (Lassen County)

The name, applied in 1850, was named for the sweetish substance, "honeydew", deposited on the plants by the aphids. Indians valued the substance as a food item.

Hoopa (Humboldt County)

The name applied to natives on the lower course of Trinity River. The name was recorded in 1852.

Hopland (Mendocino County)

The town was called Sanel until 1880. The name was changed when an experiment at growing hops was successful, prompting a change in the name.

Hornitos (Mariposa County)

(Hohr-nee-toce) The name is Spanish for "little ovens". Because of the hard and rocky soil, the Mexican miners buried their dead in aboveground tombs that resembled Mexican outdoor ovens used to bake bread.

Hueneme (Ventura County)

(wy-nee-a, wy-nee-mee) The name is derived from the Chumash Indian village *"Wene-me"*. The Coast Survey named it in 1856.

Inyo (Name of county)

(een-yoh) This is the name given by the Indians to the mountains to the Eastward. The name signifies the dwelling place of a great spirit.

Ivanpah (San Bernardino County)

The name means "good water" in the language of the Southern Piute tribe. It was applied to the railroad terminal of the Santa Fe in 1902.

Jackson (Amador County)

This town and Jacksonville (Tuolumne County) honor "Colonel Alden M. Jackson, a lawyer, generally liked by miners for settling quarrels out of court.

Jacumba (San Diego County)

(hah-kum-bah) A rancheria, *Jacom,* appears in documents in 1795. The word is believed to be Digueno Indian.

Jalama (Santa Barbara County)

(ha-lam-a) This was an Indian Chumash rancheria of La Purisma Mission in 1791.

Jamacha (San Diego County)

(ham-a-shaw) This Spanish land grant was recorded in 1831. The name is derived from Diegueno Indian *"hamacha"*, meaning a small, wild squash.

Jamestown (Tuolumne County)

A mining center in gold rush days, it was named after its founder, Col. George James, of San Francisco. It has long been familiarly known as "Jimtown".

Jamul (San Diego County)

(ha-mool) The name is from a Diegueno Indian word meaning "foam" or "lather". It was first mentioned as *Jamol* in 1776, and as *Jamul* in the 1820's.

Jayhawker Well (Death Valley)

The National Park Service gave this name to the site in 1936, honoring the Jayhawker party from Illinois, which crossed the desert in 1849 and camped there.

Jenny Lind (Calaveras County)

This town was named in a burst of enthusiasm for the Swedish Nightingale. It is now a ghost camp, marked by the remains of Sinclair's adobe store and the Rosenberg building.

Jim Crow Canyon (Sierra County)

A Hawaiian *Kanaka*, called Jim Crow as Kanakas frequently were, returned from Sacramento where he had shopped for supplies, only to find his employers gone. He worked the claim alone and struck it rich.

Johannesburg (Kern County)

Named in 1897 after the famous mining center in South Africa. It is popularly known as "Joburg".

Jolon (Monterey County)

(ho-lohn) This is an Indian name meaning the "valley of dead oaks." It may have been, at one time, A Salinan Indian rancheria. The post office was named in 1860.

Joshua Tree National Monument (San Bernardino County)

Mormons named the desert tree *(Yucca brevifolia)* the Joshua tree. It seemed a symbol of Joshua leading them to the Promised Land.

Junipero Serra Peak (Monterey County)

(huh-nip-er-oh) Junipero Serra founded nine missions in Alta California. His name was applied to the highest peak of the Santa Lucia Mountains in 1907.

Jurupa (Riverside County)

The name is of unknown meaning. It was applied to two land grants in 1838.

Kaweah (Tulare County)

(kah-wee-ah) The river system was known in 1851 as "Four Creeks", the first of which, *Cowier* or *Cahwia*, and was named for the Yokuts Indian tribe or village on its bank. In 1855, the name, spelled Kaweeyah, was given to all four of its branches.

Keeler (Inyo)

Keeler is now a ghost town. It was a terminal for the steamer ships that traversed Owens Lake from Keeler to Cartago. Keeler took all the ore from the smelter at nearby Swansea, and shipped it via either steamboat or the Carson and Colorado railroad, which ended at Keeler. The town was named in 1882 for J.M. Keeler, manager of a nearby marble quarry.

Keene (Kern County)

It was named in 1879 for the Keene family.

Kelseyville (Lake County)

It was first called "Kelsey Town" in the 1860's in memory of Andrew Kelsey, who was killed by the Indians in 1819, in revenge for his mistreatment of them.

Kern (Kern County)

John C. Fremont named the Kern River in 1845 for his topographer and artist, Edward M. Kern, of Philadelphia. The county was named in 1866.

Kettleman Hills (Kings County)

David Kettleman was a "forty-niner" and pioneer cattleman. The town was named for him.

Kiavah Mountain (Kern County)

It was named for a Piute Indian chief.

Kibesillah (Mendocino County)

The name is a Pomo Indian word meaning "flat rock". During the late 1800s the rush for redwood was on, and every nook along the Mendocino coastline had a little town and lumber mill. Kibesillah was one of the busier ports and was called the "coming metropolis of the North Coast."

Kimshew Creek (Butte County)

The name is probably from a Maidu Indian word, *ki-wim-se-u* meaning "little water".

King City (Monterey County)

Southern Pacific Railroad officials named the city in 1886 after C.H. King, owner of Rancho San Lorenzo, when the line of the railroad was extended to that point.

Kings River (Kings County)

The county was named for the river which Spanish explorers in 1805 called *"Rio de los Santos Reyes"*, (river of the holy kings). The reference is to the fact it was discovered on "Epiphany", the day of the three holy kings. The present name appeared on maps in 1850.

Klamath River (Del Norte County)

The name is derived from "Tlamatl", a name given by the Chinook Indians to a sister tribe of Modoc Indians who called themselves "Maklaks," meaning, "the encamped people." The Klamath Indian tribe, and a river in the region were mentioned as "Clammitt" in 1826. Rogue River was called "Clamouth" in 1828.

Knights Landing (Yolo County)

Both Knights Landing and Knights Ferry are named for William Knight, who settled on the Sacramento River in 1843. When gold was discovered, he operated a ferry on the Stanislaus River.

Konocti, Mount (Lake County)

The name is derived from Southeastern Pomo Indian *"kno"* (mountain) and *"hatai"* (woman). Mount Konocti dominates the Clear Lake region of northern California, just north of the Napa Valley and east of The Geysers. It has also been called Uncle Sam Mountain.

Kuna Peak (Mono County)

Named by the Geological Survey in 1883. *(kuna"* means "firewood" in the Mono Indian dialect.

Kyburz (El Dorado County)

The town was named after Albert Kyburz, son of Samuel Kyburz, a native of Switzerland, who was an important figure at Sutter's Fort before and during the gold rush.

La Canada (Los Angeles County)

The name means "canyon" or "glen". It is taken from a land grant of 1843 call *"La Canada"*.

La Crescenta (Los Angeles County)

The name was applied to the post office in 1888. There are different versions of how the name came about. Some tell the tale of the romantic Spanish lovers who, many moons ago, watched the silver crescent sink behind the Verdugo Hills; others relate that the name came from the fact that the Valley forms a crescent around the base of the mountains.

Lafayette (Contra Costa County)

The settlement was named in 1853. Like many others in the U.S., it honors the French general who fought in the American War for Independence.

La Grange (Stanislaus County)

The name dates back to 1882 when it was first founded as a mining camp. At one time, it was the county seat. Author Bret Harte taught school there.

La Habra (Orange County)

(hah-bra) It derives its name from *"abra"*, which means "canyon" or "gorge". The name was used on a land grant dated October 22, 1839.

La Jolla (San Diego County)

(Lah Ho-yah) The Spanish word *"joya"* means, "jewel". The word *"hoya"* is a Mexican geographical term for hollow, pit, or riverbed. The name appears in mission and land grant records since 1828, and was applied to the town in 1869.

La Mirada (Los Angeles County)

The Santa Fe Railroad station was given this name in 1888. In Spanish, *"Mirada"* means "glance" or "gaze".

Lassen (Lassen County)

Named for Peter Lassen, a Danish trailblazer who arrived in the Northeastern California region in 1839. Both Lassen Peak and Lassen Volcanic National Park are named for the pathfinder.

Lebec (Kern County)

Named for Peter Lebeck, who was killed by a grizzly in 1837. His name was inscribed on an oak and was first mentioned in 1847.

Leevining (Mono County)

(lee-vy-ning) Named for Leroy Vining, who came to California in 1852, and later operated a sawmill at the creek.

Lembert Dome (Yosemite National Park)

Name in 1885 for John B. Lembert, who homesteaded land near the glaciated dome.

Lemoore (Kings County)

First known as Lee Moore's, for Dr. L. Lee Moore. The Southern Pacific changed it to its present form in the 1880's.

Leucadia (San Diego County)

English settlers in 1885 gave the town the name of one of the Ionian Islands, located in the Ionian Sea.

Likely (Modoc County)

As the story goes, when settlers tried to find a name for the post office in 1878, one of them said, "Wa'al, we're likely to find a name and we're likely not to." The emphasis on the adverb captured the group's fancy and they selected it as the name.

Linda (Yuba County)

Named in 1850 for the first steamer launched on the Sacramento River.

Lindsay (Tulare County)

The name was given the Southern Pacific station in 1869 for Mrs. A.J. Hutchinson, whose maiden name was "Lindsay".

Livermore (Alameda County)

It was named for Robert Livermore, an English sailor, and the first English-speaking settler in the Livermore Valley. He settled in the valley in the 1820's.

Llagas Creek (Santa Clara County)

(yah-gas) It was named *"Las Llagas de Nuestro Padre San Francisco,"* (the wounds of our father Saint Francis) by Palou in 1774.

Lobos, Point (San Francisco County)

This, and other communities carrying the *"Lobos"* name, which means "wolves", generally refers to the *"lobo marino"*, (sea wolf, seal).

Lodi (San Joaquin County)

Named in 1874, this is one of twenty other Lodi's listed in the United States. A famous racehorse by that name in the 1870's may have influenced the naming.

Loma, Lomita

Spanish for "low hill", the name is often used without regard to meaning, for mountains as well as subdivisions.

Lompoc (Santa Barbara County)

The name was given to a Chumash Indian rancheria in 1791. The name means, "shell mound".

Long Beach (Los Angeles County)

Just 50 years after Columbus discovered America, Cabrillo and his crew of explorers anchored off the present site of Long Beach. Vast clouds of smoke were rolling high in the sky from burning grass. Ashore, the native Indians were conducting one of their periodic rabbit drives. Cabrillo named the area *"Bahia de los Fumos"* (the Bay of Smokes). The first modern identity for Long Beach began with the sprawling rancho awarded Manuel Nieto in 1784. Time and descendants divided the old Spanish Land Grant until the bulk of what is now Long Beach was contained in two ranchos, Los Cerritos and Los Alamitos.

Los Altos (Santa Clara County)

The term, in Spanish, means "the heights". It was given the post office in 1908.

Los Angeles (Los Angeles County)

(Loce Ahn-hay-lace) Its full name was, *"El Pueblo de Nuestra Senora de la Reina de los Angeles de la Porcinuncula",* (the town of Our Lady the Queen of the Angels of Portiuncula." Portiuncula was the chapel in Assissi, Italy, cradle of the Franciscan Order. The county and the city became officially Los Angeles in 1850.

Los Banos (Merced County)

The name, in Spanish, means "the baths." In early days, Padre Felipe Arroyo de la Cuesta of Mission San Juan Bautista, used to refresh himself when on missionary trips, in the pools of Los Banos Creek. They were called *"Los Banos del Padre Arroyo."* Gustav Kreyenhagen, who established the town, applied the name of the creek to the town about 1868.

Los Coches (Santa Barbara County)

(koh-ches) Named for the herds of wild hogs that had escaped from the missions during Mexican times.

Los Gatos (Santa Clara County)

(Loce Gah-toce) The name, in Spanish, means, "The cats." It was originally called, *"La Rinconada de los Gatos"*, the rendezvous of the wildcats, which infested the region. The post office was named Los Gatos in 1864.

Los Osos (San Luis Obispo County)

(Loce Oh-soce) In Spanish, the name means "The Bears. On Portola's trek from San Diego to Monterey, his soldiers were awed when they sighted grizzly bears digging for roots and grubs. They were able to kill and cook one bear. The locale became the site of Mission San Luis Obispo.

Los Padres National Forest

Named in 1936 to commemorate the Franciscan padres, eight of whose missions are in or near the forest reserve.

Los Penasquitos Canyon (San Diego County)

(pen-as-kee-tos) The name, which, in Spanish, means "small rocks", can be found in the land grant, *"Santa Maria de los Penasquitos*, June 15, 1823.

Lost Hills (Kern County)

The town was named in 1910 after the slight elevations which seemed to belong to the "Kettleman Hills", but which looked as if they were "lost."

Lucerne Valley (San Bernardino County)

The name is derived from the European word for alfalfa.

Ludlow (San Bernardino County)

This desert stop was named by the railroad in 1870 for William B. Ludlow, a master car repairer.

Lynwood (Los Angeles County)

The town was named for Lynn Wood Sessions, the wife of the owner of a local dairy.

McCloud (Siskiyou County)

In 1829, a party of Hudson Bay Company trappers and explorers, led by Peter Skeen Ogden and Alexander Roderick McLeod, were the first white men to travel through the valley where McCloud now stands.

Madera (Madera County)

(ma-dehr-a) The name is the Spanish word for "wood, timber or lumber". It was so-named because it was the end of a 63-mile flume carrying lumber from Soquel Basin in the Sierra sugar-pine forests. The county was created in 1893 and named after the town.

Mad River (Humboldt and Trinity counties)

The name arose because of a dispute by members of the Gregg surveying party. Men in the party became "mad" and refused to wait for their leader, Dr. Josiah Gregg, to take the latitude of the river's mouth.

Malibu (Los Angeles County)

The present spelling is found on an 1805 Topanga Malibu land grant. The name is probably the Chumash Indian rancheria *"Umalibo"*, in the jurisdiction of Mission San Buenaventura.

Manteca (San Joaquin County)

The railroad station was named in 1870 after a local creamery, which was appropriately named, *"Manteca"*, Spanish for "butter".

Manzanita

(man-za-nee-ta) This is a beautiful shrub that graces much of California's wild lands. In Spanish, it means "little apple."

Mare Island (Solano County)

Legend has it that the island, once known as *Isla Plana*, got its present name when one of General Mariano Guadalupe Vallejo's prize mares fell overboard while being ferried across the bay. It was thereafter called *"Isla de la Yegua'*, (Mare Island).

Maricopa (Kern County)

When Southern Pacific Railroad extended its line, the terminus was called "Maricopa", after the Indian tribe that lives on the Gila River in Arizona.

Marin (Marin County)

Spanish pronunciation is "Mah-rinn". It is taken from *El Marinero* (the sailor). A San Francisco exploring party had a desperate fight with the Licatiut tribe in Petaluma and captured its chief. He was subsequently converted to Christianity and did such good service in navigating the bay that he was called *"El Marinero."*

Mariposa (Mariposa County)

(Mah-ree-poh-sah) The Spanish word for butterfly, it got its name from an expedition led by Alferez Gabriel Moraga. The exploring party encountered hordes of the colorful butterflies as it crossed the San Joaquin River.

Markleeville (Alpine County)

The post office was named in 1864 for Jacob J. Marklee, a settler in the area.

Martinez (Contra Costa County)

It was named for Ignacio Martinez, *commandante* at the Presidio of San Francisco, 1822-1827. He was granted Rancho El Pinole in 1829, the site on which the town was built.

Marysville (Yuba County)

The name was unanimously chosen at a mass meeting of pioneers to honor Mary Murphy Covillaud, a survivor of the Donner Party and wife of the man who laid out the town in 1849-1850.

Massacre Canyon (Riverside County)

Temecula Indians massacred a band of Ivahs here for the possession of a supply of wild grain.

Mather

The station in Tuolumne County, the pass in Fresno County, and the grove in Humboldt County were all named for Stephen T. Mather, first director of the National Park Service.

Mecca (Riverside County)

It is only one of several Meccas in the United States that resembles the Arabian city in climate and surroundings.

Melones (Calaveras County)

Spanish miners named this gold camp for the coarse nuggets they found there that resembled melon seeds. The town was once called "Slumgullion".

Mendocino (Mendocino County)

(Mayn-doh-see-noh) The name is derived from the name given Cape Mendocino by Juan Rodriguez Cabrillo in 1542 in honor of Don Antonio Mendoza, first viceroy of New Spain (Mexico).

Mendota (Fresno County)

The railroad station was named in 1895, probably after one of the Mendotas in the east.

Menlo Park (San Mateo County)

It was named after Menlough, county Galway, Ireland, in 1854 by settlers from Ireland.

Merced (Merced County)

Captain Gabriel Moraga named the river *"El Rio de Nuestra Senora de la Merced,"* "the river of our Lady of Mercy" (The Virgin Mary). The name was chosen because of the joy the exploring party felt over its refreshing waters after trekking forty miles through waterless country.

Meridian (Sutter County)

It gained its name in 1860 because of its proximity to the Mount Diablo meridian.

Merritt, Lake (Alameda County)

Because of his efforts, a slough was turned into a lake in 1869. It was named in honor of Mayor Samuel B. Merritt in 1891.

Mesa (San Diego County)

(may-sa) Mesa is the Spanish word for a "flat-topped hill". There are more than twenty towns incorporating *Mesa* in their names.

Millbrae (San Mateo County)

The name was given the railroad station in the 1860's. It was named after the country place of Darius O. Mills, a leading banker and promoter of San Francisco and New York.

Mill Valley (Marin County)

It got its name from the fact that a sawmill was built there in 1834.

Milpitas (Santa Clara County)

(mil-pee-tas) In Spanish, the word means "vegetable gardens". The town was named after the Milpitas land grant of 1835. The name was first applied to a nearby creek, where some Indians maintained a truck garden.

Modesto (Stanislaus County)

When William C. Ralston, a director of the Central Pacific Railroad, modestly declined to have his name used for the station, the Spanish adjective for the word "modest" was chosen instead.

Modoc County

The county was named for the Modoc Indian tribe, which had been beaten in the Modoc War. The word comes from the Klamath Indian name *"Moatokni"*, which means "people living south."

Mohave (San Bernardino County)

The name is derived from an Indian tribe in the region where California, Arizona, and Nevada meet.

Mojave (San Bernardino County)

(Moh-hah-vay) An Arizona tribal Indian name, meaning "the people who live on the Colorado River near Needles." The Arizona spelling for this name is "Mohave".

Mokelumne Hill (Calaveras County)

Mokelumne Hill got its name from the Mokelumne River, which itself was named after a Miwok Indian village located on the river.

Mono (County and Lake)

The name is a corruption of Monache or Monachi (Chi: tribe or division), the appellation given these Shoshonean Indians by the Miwok and Yokuts Indians. The word Monachi means, "fly people", as these Indians lived on the pupae of flies.

Montecito (Santa Barbara County)

The name means "little grove, or woods". It was applied to a land grant in 1834.

Monterey (Monterey County)

Sebastian Vizcaino named the village in honor of Gaspar de Zuniga, Count of Monterey and Viceroy of Mexico. In 1776, Monterey was declared the cap ital of Baja and Alta California during the Spanish regime. The name has been variously spelled in the past as Monterrey and Monte Rey.

Moraga (Contra Costa County)

(Moh-rah-gah) Moraga is the surname of Gabriel Moraga, a Spanish explorer. His son, Joaquin

Moraga in 1835 was the co-grantee of the rancho on which the station is situated.

Moreno (Riverside County)

It was named for F.E. Brown, one of the developers. When he refused to have his name used for the town, the name was translated into Spanish and used anyway.

Morgan Hill (Santa Clara County)

Named after Morgan Hill, on whose ranch the town is located.

Moro Rock (Sequoia National Park)

Mexican Californians used the term *"moro"* for "blue roan." The rock is named for a mustang that often ranged under the rock.

Morro (San Luis Obispo County)

The names of the region are derived from Morro Rock, at the entrance of the bay, which in Spanish mean "round rock or round-topped hill".

Murphys (Calaveras County)

Named for John Murphy, an immigrant of 1844. Mining claims were so rich there that claims were limited to eight-square-feet. John Murphy was said to have reaped $1,500,000 from his Murphys Diggings claim.

Naciemiento River (Monterey and San Luis Obispo counties)

In Spanish, the name means "source of a river". Juan Bautista de Anza camped by the stream on April 16, 1774, and called it Naciemiento.

Napa (Napa County)

The name is all that is left of the Napa Indians who were virtually exterminated by smallpox in 1838. Many meanings have been advanced for the name, including "harpoon point, fish, abundant, and near home."

National City (San Diego County)

It is named for the *Rancho de la Nacion* on which the town is laid out. Until Mexican independence (1822) it had been called Rancho del Rey (the king's ranch)

Natoma (Sacramento County)

This is an Indian name indicating direction, such as "upstream". One translation gives the meaning as "the girl from the mountains."

Needles (San Bernardino County)

When a railroad station was established on the Arizona side of the Colorado River in February 1883, it was given the name of Needles after the nearby pinnacles. The name was transferred to the California side in October of 1883.

Nevada City (Nevada County)

Nevada is the Spanish word meaning "snow covered", and was applied to the town in 1850. The town was named before the state of Nevada adopted the name.

Newport (Orange County)

The town was named after a boat owned by the McFadden brothers, developers of the town.

New River (Imperial County)

Immigrants named the river in 1849 when they came unexpectedly on a stream which expeditions of the preceding years had listed as a dry riverbed, but which was now filled with overflow from the Colorado River.

Nipomo (San Luis Obispo County)

A Chumash Indian rancheria, *"Nipoma"*, was recorded in 1799. The present spelling was later used on a land grant in 1837.

Nojogui (Santa Barbara County)

Mentioned as a rancheria in mission records, the name may go back to a Chumash Indian word.

Norco (Riverside County)

The name is abbreviated from the name of the North Corona Land Company.

Norwalk (Los Angeles County)

The town was named in 1879 after the hometown of settlers from Connecticut.

Novato (Marin County)

(No-vah-toh) The name is listed in land grants of 1836. It is used as both the name of a town and of a valley. One authority says the name is derived from that of a chief of the Hookooeko Indians who probably had been baptized for Novatus, early Roman Christian.

Oakland (Alameda County)

It was once called "*Las Encinas*", the Spanish name for "oak grove." The present name was chosen when the city was laid out in 1850.

Ocotillo (San Diego County)

The town is named after the cactus-like plant. It is derived from the Aztec root meaning "prickly".

Ojai (Ventura County)

The name comes from the Chumash Indian name *"A'hwai"*, meaning, "moon". A rancheria *"Aujai"* is mentioned in mission records.

Olancha (Inyo County)

It is named for the Olanchas, a Shoshonean Indian group south of Owens Lake.

Ontario (San Bernardino County)

George B. Chaffey, who came from Ontario, Canada, laid out the town in 1882, and named it for his hometown.

Ophir (Placer County)

It is named after Ophir, the gold land in the Bible and is the only one of five mining towns once named Ophir to survive.

Orange (Orange County)

The city was founded in 1873, and was probably named after its chief citrus product.

Orinda (Contra Costa County)

The name was the pen name of Katherine Fowler Philips, an English poetess.

Orosi (Tulare County)

(oh-roh-sye) The name is coined from the Spanish *"oro"*, which means "gold". It was given to the town in 1888.

Oroville (Butte County)

The riverbed on which Oroville was built was rich in gold, and a dredging company once offered to move the entire town for the right to mine the ground underneath it. *"Oro"* is the Spanish word for gold.

Otay (San Diego County)

A rancheria by this name is mentioned as early as 1776. In 1829 and 1846 the name was applied to a land grant. The name was given to the river in 1849. The name is a Diegueno Indian word meaning "brushy".

Oxnard (Ventura County)

The city was named for Henry T. Oxnard, who established a sugar refinery there in 1897.

Pacheco (Contra Costa County)

(Pay-chay-coh) The town is named for Salvio Pacheco, who settled on Monte del Diablo Rancho in 1844. Pacheco Pass was named for another Pacheco family.

Pacifica (San Mateo County)

In 1957, nine communities incorporated as a city and chose the name for their contiguity to the ocean shore.

Pacific Grove (Monterey County)

In 1875, a group of Methodists organized under the name Pacific Grove Retreat Association to establish a seaside resort on land in the pine grove west of Monterey. That site today is the site of the city.

Paicines (San Benito County)

It was named after the Indian village *"Paisi-n"* in 1874.

Pajaro (Monterey County)

(Pah-hah-roh) The name, in Spanish, means bird. Portola's soldiers, who found an enormous bird there, which Indians had stuffed with straw, applied the name to the Pajaro River.

Pala (San Diego County)

(pah-lah) It was first mentioned as a rancheria in 1781. The name may mean "water" in Luiseno Shoshonean Indian.

Palo Alto (Santa Clara County)

The name, which means high tree, was given to the redwood tree by Don Gaspar de Portola's advance guard in 1769.

Panamint (Inyo County)

Name is derived from a division of Shoshonean Indians who occupied the region, possibly the *"Benemes"*, mentioned in 1861.

Paraiso (Monterey County)

The Spanish word for "Paradise", this is the only survivor of several places that once carried the name.

Pasadena (Los Angeles County)

Stockholders of the Indiana Colony adopted the name in 1875. It was taken from the language of the Chippewa Indians of the Mississippi Valley, and means, "valley".

Paso Robles (San Luis Obispo County)

The town was founded in 1886 with the name, *"El Paso de Robles"*, (pass of the oaks). Anza's expedition mentioned the numerous oaks, and in 1844, the name, *"Paso de Robles"* was applied to a land grant.

Patterson (Stanislaus County)

The community was named for John D. Patterson, who purchased the land in 1864.

Pauma (San Diego County)

This was a rancheria of the Luiseno Indians. The name was applied to a land grant in 1844.

Penryn (Placer County)

The community is named after a city in Wales (Penrhyn). The name was given to the railroad station in the 1870's.

Perris (Riverside County)

The town was named in 1886 for Fred T. Perris, chief engineer for California Southern Railroad.

Pescadero (San Mateo County)

(Pace-cah-day-roh) The name is Spanish for "fishing place."

Petaluma (Sonoma County)

This is a coast Miwok Indian name meaning "flat-back", a term that is descriptive of a hill near the present city of Petaluma. It was applied to a land grant in 1851.

Picacho Peak (Imperial County)

This is the Spanish word for peak. When applied, as it is in this situation, the name literally means "peak, peak".

Pico (Los Angeles County)

The community was named for California's last Mexican governor, Pio Pico.

Pinole (Contra Costa County)

The name comes from the Mexican word for meal made from grain or seed. It was used as early as 1775 by Spaniards telling of food made by the Indians in the district. The name was given to a land grant in 1823.

Piru (Ventura County)

This is an Indian name of Shoshonean origin, recorded in 1817.

Pismo (San Luis Obispo County)

A Chumash Indian name that probably means "tar"; it was applied to a land grant in 1840.

Pit River (Northeastern California)

It was so-named because Indians living along the river dug conical pits, with a small opening at the top, to trap animals. The openings were covered with brush to hide them. Sharp stakes or deer antlers were often placed in the bottom of the pits to impale the prey.

Pittsburg (Contra Costa County)

This community's first name was "New York of the Pacific", bestowed in 1849 when William Tecumseh Sherman laid out the town site for Col. Jonathan D. Stevenson of the First New York Volunteers. The name was changed in the 1850's after coal deposits were found near Mt. Diablo, to "Black Diamond." Later on, when manufacturing possibilities loomed, it was changed to Pittsburg, after Pittsburg, Pennsylvania.

Placentia (Orange County)

The name was first given to a school district, possibly after the town in Newfoundland, and then transferred to the town in 1910.

Placer (County)

This is a western term of Spanish origin for deposits containing gold particles obtainable by washing.

Placerville (El Dorado County)

It was first called "Old Dry Diggings" and later "Hangtown" when it was the first mining community with a recorded lynching in the Mother Lode.

Pleasanton (Alameda County)

The town was named in 1867 for General Alfred Pleasonton, an often-cited officer in the Mexican and Civil wars. The name has been misspelled since the 1870's.

Plumas County

Created in 1854, the county is so-named because it is drained by the Feather River which was called "*Rio de las Plumas*" during California's Mexican period. (See Feather River)

Pomona (Los Angeles County)

The name for the Roman goddess of orchards was given to the city in 1875.

Porterville (Tulare County)

Porter Putnam, in 1864, laid out the town and brazenly named it for himself.

Poway (San Diego County)

The name is derived from Paguay, and was mentioned as a rancho in 1828, in a land grant in 1839, and was applied to an arroyo in 1841.

Puente (Los Angeles County)

(Poo-en-te) Portola mentioned a *"Llano de la Puente"* in 1770. The expedition built a bridge of poles in order to cross an arroyo. In 1842, the name was applied to the Puente de San Gabriel land grant.

Putah Creek (Napa, Solano counties)

(poo-ta) The stream preserves the name of a branch of Patwin Indians who once dwelt on its banks. It's similarity to the Spanish word *"puta"*, which means "harlot", is purely accidental.

Quincy (Plumas County)

When the town became the seat of Plumas County in 1854, it was named after Quincy, Illinois, the hometown of the owner of the hotel.

Ramona (San Diego County)

Helen Hunt Jackson's popular novel "Ramona" lent its name to several communities in the late 1880's.

Rancho Cordova (Sacramento County)

This is a relatively new community, developed in 1955. It was named after the Cordova Vineyards on the *Rancho de los Americanos* grant.

Rancho Santa Fe (San Diego County)

In October of 1906, the Santa Fe Land and Improvement Company, a subsidiary of the Santa Fe Railroad, purchased all of the lands that made up the original 'San Dieguito Land Grant. The Santa Fe Railroad's intent was to use the rancho lands to produce wood from Eucalyptus trees for railroad ties. The ranch later was sold for a subdivision.

Randsburg (Kern County)

The Rand Mountain gold strike of the 1890's was one of the biggest for California, large enough to create a town and bring in a stage line from Mojave.

Red Bluff (Tehama County)

It was named in 1850 after the fifty-foot reddish bluff overlooking the Sacramento River.

Redding (Shasta County)

The town was named after B.B. Redding, land agent of the Central Pacific, in 1872.

Redlands (San Bernardino County)

It was named in 1887 for its reddish soil.

Redondo Beach (Los Angeles County)

Founded in 1881, the town was apparently named after the adjoining *Rancho Sausal Redondo* (round willow grove).

Redwood City (San Mateo County)

In the 1850's this city was the embarcadero or shipping point for redwood lumber. The lumber was cut in the mountains to the west, and used in the building of San Francisco.

Reedley (Fresno County)

The town is named for Thomas L. Reed. When Reed donated half of his holdings to the city in 1888, he declined having the town named after him. The city fathers simply added a suffix (ley).

Refugio Pass (Santa Barbara County)

The name appears in the land grant *"Nuestra Senora del Refugio"* (Our Lady of the Refuge) of 1794, and was recorded in later years in the abbreviated form.

Rialto (San Bernardino County)

The name is a shortened version of "Rivus Altus", the name of the Grand Canal of Venice.

Richmond (Contra Costa County)

The community's name was derived from Point Richmond, San Francisco Bay, which was named for Richmond, Virginia, the birthplace of Edmund Randolph. Randolph represented San Francisco at the first session of the California legislature in San Jose in 1849. He was the son of Governor Edmund Randolph, of Virginia.

Rio Vista (Solano County)

The Spanish name for "river view", this Sacramento River town was earlier called *"Brazos del Rio"*. Brazos is Spanish for "arms".

Ripon (San Joaquin County)

Named in 1876 by Applias Crooks, the first post master, for Ripon, Wisconsin, his former home and the birthplace of the Republican Party.

Riverside (Riverside County)

Its name is founded in the city's proximity to the Santa Ana River. The city was named in 1871, and the county was named in 1893.

Roseville (Placer County)

A popular American place name, it was given to the Central Pacific station in 1864. According to one story, picnicking residents named the town after the most popular girl present. A more popular story is that it was given this name simply because of its pleasant sound.

Rough and Ready (Nevada County)

It was a wild and scandalous town during the gold rush. It was founded by a group of Mexican War veterans who decided to name their tent city after their ex-commander, General Zachary "Old Rough and Ready" Taylor. It is now essentially a ghost town.

Rubidoux, Mount (Riverside County)

Named for Louis Rubidoux in 1844. He was one-time owner of Rancho Jurupa.

Russian River (Sonoma County)

The Russians occupied the territory between Bodega Bay and Fort Ross from 1812 to 1841, and called the river *"Slavianka"*. The Spanish called it *"San Ignacio,* and also, *"Rio Ruso"*. The present name came into use after American occupation.

Sacramento (Sacramento County)

Captain Moraga first christened the river from which the city gets its name "Jesus Maria". A branch was called Sacramento. Later this name was applied to the main stream. The Spanish name, "Holy Sacrament", was applied to the Feather River in 1808. It was later assumed that the lower Sacramento was the same stream. In 1817, the two main rivers of the valley were recorded as Sacramento and San Joaquin rivers.

Salinas (Monterey County)

(sa-lee-nas) It was named for the *"salinas"* (salt marshes) near the mouth of the river. The name was also used for a land grant before 1795, but it was not in general use for the river until 1846. The name of the city is recorded in 1860.

Salton Sea (Riverside and Imperial Counties)

The lakebed was named in 1892 after the Southern Pacific station on its shore. The name was kept and applied to the lake that formed when the Colorado River broke its levees in 1907.

San Andreas (Calaveras County)

This former mining camp was settled and named by Mexican miners in 1848.

San Anselmo (Marin County)

(an-sel-mo) *Canada de Anselmo* appears in the papers of the *Punta de Quintin* grant of 1840. It was applied to the North Pacific Railroad station in the 1890's.

San Ardo (Monterey County)

Many think this community is named after a saint, but it's not. The name is abbreviated from San Bernardo to avoid confusion with San Bernardino.

San Benito (San Benito County)

It was named in 1772 for St. Benedict, founder of the Benedictine Order. In 1842, the name was given to a land grant an in 1874, applied to the county.

San Bernardino (San Bernardino County)

This town was named for an Italian saint. In 1842, the name was applied to a land grant. Mormons established a settlement on a part of the grant in 1851, which is now part of the present city.

San Bruno (San Mateo County)

Francisco Palou, a friar who worked with the missions, gave the name of a German saint of the 11th century to a creek in 1774, *Sierra de San Bruno* (San Bruno Mountains). The San Bruno House, the nucleus of the town, existed in 1862.

San Buenaventura (Ventura County)

Mission San Buenaventura was the ninth and last mission established by Father Junipero Serra. The padres taught the Indians to dam up water and build canals. Buenaventura was sometimes called *"the place of the canals."*

San Carlos (San Mateo County)

It was named in 1887 for St. Charles Borromeo, Archbishop of Milan. It was thought that the Portola expedition first saw San Francisco Bay from the hills behind San Carlos on November 4, 1769, the feast day of St. Charles.

San Clemente Island (Los Angeles County)

Sebastian Vizcaino named this island in honor of St. Clement. The town in Orange County was named after the island.

San Diego (San Diego County.

Sebastian Vizcaino named the Bay in 1602 in honor of Saint Didacus of Alcala, a Franciscan saint of the 15th century. The mission was named in 1769 and the name was applied to the county in 1850, and to the city in 1856.

San Dimas

The community started out in the early 1800s being called Mud Springs, named for the adjacent Mud Springs marsh. The town was formally put on the map in 1887, the year the Santa Fe Railroad was completed and began operating a rail line through the area.

San Fernando (Los Angeles County)

The Mission was established in 1797 and named in honor of Saint Ferdinand, King of Castile and Leon in the 13th century. The City was named in 1874.

San Francisco (San Francisco County)

Bahia de San Francisco was the name given in honor of Saint Francis of Assissi to what is now Drakes Bay. For 174 years, the name remained a vague geographical conception until a detachment of the Portola expedition, searching for Monterey Bay, beheld the large body of water between them and Point Reyes. They thought they were looking on the original bay or port of San Francisco.

San Gabriel (Los Angeles County)

The river was known by this name before 1782. The town was given the name in 1771. It is named for the Archangel Gabriel.

Sanger (Fresno County)

Southern Pacific Railroad gave the name to a railroad station in 1888 in honor of Joseph Sanger, an official with the line.

San Gorgonio (Riverside County)

This name was given to a cattle ranch of the San Gabriel Mission before 1824. In 1843, a land grant was named *San Jacinto y San Gorgonio*. The pass and the mountains have been known by this name since the early 1850's.

San Jacinto (Riverside County)

(ja-sin-toh) In the 1840's the name *San Jacinto* (Saint Hyacinth) was applied to three land grants, and in 1872 the name was given to the town. *San Jacinto Viejo* was a cattle ranch of Mission San Luis Rey in 1821.

San Joaquin

This is the name of both a county and a river. The name comes from St. Joachim, father of the Virgin Mary. Gabriel Moraga named the river in 1806. The county was named after the river in 1850.

San Jose (Santa Clara County)

(sahn hoh-say) The *pueblo*, the first in Upper California, was founded in 1777. It was named for Saint Joseph, husband of the Virgin Mary. San Jose is the most popular saint's name in Spanish-speaking countries.

San Juan Bautista (San Benito County)

The post office was originally called San Juan, but was later changed to the complete form. The mission was named in 1797 for Saint John the Baptist.

San Juan Capistrano (Orange County)

(san wahn kap-i-strah-noh) The mission was named in 1776 in honor of Saint John Capistran, the fighting priest of the 15th century who took a heroic part in the defense of Vienna against the Turks.

San Leandro (Alameda County)

It was named in 1855 after a land grant, *Arroyo de San Leandro* (creek of Saint Leander), which was mentioned in records in 1828.

San Lorenzo (Alameda County)

The two "Saint Lawrence land grants (1841, 1842) were apparently named after the *Arroyo de San Lorenzo* (now San Lorenzo Creek).

San Lucas (Monterey County)

It was named after the *Rancho San Lucas*, granted in 1842. The land grant was named for Saint Luke. The town was founded in 1886.

San Luis Obispo (San Luis Obispo County)

The mission was founded 1772 and named for Louis, Bishop of Toulouse, and a 13th-century saint. The city and the county were both named after the mission in 1850.

San Luis Rey (San Diego County)

The name is derived from the mission established in 1798. The mission was named for Saint Louis, King of France.

San Marcos (San Diego County)

El Valle S. Marcos (Saint Mark's valley) was used for a land grant.

San Marino (Los Angeles County)

James de Barth Shorb, who built a home on the site in 1878, named the town. He named it San Marino after his home in Maryland.

San Martin (Santa Clara County)

Martin Murphy, an 1844 immigrant, named the town for his patron saint.

San Mateo (San Mateo County)

Named for Saint Matthew, the county was created in 1856. It was once a part of San Francisco County.

San Pablo (Contra Costa County)

Early nineteenth century mapmakers named Point San Pablo and Point San Pedro on opposite sides of San Pablo Strait. It was named Saint Paul.

San Pedro (Los Angeles County)

Saint Peter was a favorite for place names in Spanish times. It has survived in a number of geographical features. The bay in Los Angeles

County was named by the Vizcaino expedition in 1602.

San Quentin (Marin County)

It was not named in honor of the saint, but only for his namesake, a notorious Indian renegade, "Quintin", who was captured in 1824. Americans added the "San" later.

San Rafael (Marin County)

(ra-fell) The mission was named *La Mission de San Rafael Arcangel* after the guardian angel of humanity. In 1851, the post office was named after the mission.

San Ramon (Contra Costa County)

The creek was named in the 1830's for a caretaker of Mission San Jose. Several land grants later carried the name.

San Simeon (San Luis Obispo County)

The name honors Saint Simon, and was the name of a rancho of Mission San Miguel recorded in 1819 and again in 1827.

Santa Ana (Orange County)

Soldiers in Portola's expedition named the river on July 28, 1769 for the feast day of Saint Anne, mother of the Virgin Mary, which they had celebrated two days previous. The name later appeared in mission records. The city was founded and named in 1869.

Santa Anita (Los Angeles County)

E.J. "Lucky" Baldwin purchased the *Santa Anita* land grant that was recorded in 1841. Baldwin built Santa Anita racetrack. Baldwin Hills and Baldwin Park are named after him.

Santa Barbara (Santa Barbara County)

Explorer Sebastian Vizcaino named the channel *"La Canal de Santa Barbara"* on December 4, 1602. He named it after the Roman maiden who was beheaded by her father for becoming a Christian. Both the city and the county were given the name in 1850.

Santa Clara (Santa Clara County)

When the mission was established in 1777, it was named for the founder of the Franciscan order of Poor Clares. The town later was named after the mission.

Santa Cruz (Santa Cruz County)

The Portola Expedition named a creek near the present city *Arroyo de Santa Cruz* (Holy Cross Creek) in 1769. In 1791, *La Mission de la Exaltacion de la Santa Cruz* was established. A settlement was founded near the mission in 1797 and called *Villa de Branciforte,* which was later changed to Santa Cruz.

Santa Margarita (San Luis Obispo County)

Juan Bautista de Anza mentioned the name in 1776. It was apparently applied before 1790 to a place where San Luis Obispo Mission raised hogs. The name honors the holy Margaret of Cortona.

Santa Maria (Santa Barbara County)

The name of the mother Jesus was often used for place names in Spanish and Mexican times.

Santa Monica (Los Angeles County)

The name appears in 1839 in the land grant *San Vicente y Santa Monica,* on which the city was founded in 1822.

Santa Paula (Ventura County)

The city is built on a land grant, *Rancho Santa Paula y Saticoy,* which was granted in 1834 and 1840.

Santa Rosa (Sonoma County)

The city is named for Saint Rose of Lima, said to be the only canonized woman saint of the New World. Luther Burbank started his famous experimental gardens here in 1878.

Santa Ynez (Santa Barbara County)

(ee-nez) The town was named in 1882 after the Mission, *Santa Ines, Virgen y Martir,* which was founded in 1804.

Santa Ysabel (San Diego County)

In 1844, the name was applied to a land grant and to an Indian reservation in 1875. It probably honors Saint Elizabeth, Queen of Portugal.

San Ysidro (San Diego County)

(ee-see-droh) The name of Saint Isadore, of the 7th Century, was given to the mountain and to an Indian rancheria in Spanish times. It was given to the town in 1909.

Saticoy (Ventura County)

There was a Chumash Indian settlement with the same spelling mentioned in a letter of May 20, 1826. The town is located on the *Santa Paula y Saticoy* land grant of 1834. The name was given to the town in 1861.

Sausalito (Marin County)

(saw-sa-lee-to) In Spanish, the name means "little willow grove". The misspelling *"Saucelito"* was used in the 1850's, was transferred to the new town in 1868, and persisted sporadically until after 1900.

Sebastopol (Sonoma County)

The name of Sebastopol first came into use in the late 1850's as a result of a prolonged and lively fistfight in the newly formed town. The brawl was likened to the long British siege of the Russian seaport of Sevastopol during the then-raging Crimean War. Britain, France, Sardinia and Turkey fought Russia in this war, one of the first wars to be directly reported by journalists and photographers. There were four Sebastopol's mentioned in 1854. This is the only survivor of the four.

Selma (Fresno County)

The naming of Selma was one of many arguments and frustrations. Several names had been submitted as a name, including "Whitson", "Erwin", "Crocker", "Dalton," "Weymouth", and "Sandwich". All were rejected for one conflict or another. Sanford Kingsbury, an assistant to Central Pacific general superintendent A.N. Towne, apparently named the town. He submitted the name of his wife, "Selma", which was eventually chosen from those offered.

Shafter (Kern County)

The town was named in memory of William ("Pecos Bill") Shafter, commander of the U.S. forces in Cuba during the Spanish-American War.

Shaver Lake (Fresno County)

It was first recorded as "Saver Lake" by the Whitney Survey on its maps of 1873. It was changed in the early 1890's when C.B. Shaver built a sawmill there.

Shoshone (Inyo County)

The railroad station was given this name in the early 1900's. It may be the only place in California named for the widespread family of Shoshonean Indians.

Sierra

This is the Spanish generic name for a saw-toothed mountain range. Sierra Nevada means the "Snowy Sierra" or the "Sierra White as Snow". The Sierra Madre is the "Mother Sierra", so-called because it was at first thought that the other outstanding ranges stemmed from this range of Southern California.

Siskiyou

This mountain pass is named from a Cree Indian word, *sisikiyawatim,* meaning "spotted horse". In 1828, Archibald R. McLeod of Hudson's Bay Company lost a "bob-tailed horse" while cross the mountains. His Canadian followers named the place, "Pass of the Siskiyou."

Smith River (Del Norte County)

Mountain Man Jedediah Smith's name was given the Lower Klamath River in 1828. The name was transferred to the present river in 1851.

Solano

(Soh-lah-noh) This is a Spanish word, meaning "easterly wind." It is also the surname of Francisco Solano, a celebrated missionary.

Soledad (Monterey County)

(sol-e-dad) The Portola expedition applied the name because the name of an Indian sounded to them like "Soledad." The mission was founded in 1791. Soledad is the Spanish word for "solitude", and has been used in several localities.

Solvang (Santa Barbara County)

In Danish, the name means "sunny meadow". It was given to this Danish colony in 1910.

Sonoma (Sonoma County)

This is an Indian word meaning "Valley of the Moon" or "Valley of Many Moons." The California Bear Flag was raised here in 1846. Don Mariano Guadalupe Vallejo founded the town.

Sonora (Tuolumne County)

The town was named for the Mexican state of Sonora, from which the first group of Mexican settlers came during the gold rush. The original name given it was "Sonorian Camp".

Stockton (San Joaquin County)

Charles M. Weber, founder of the town, named it for Commodore Robert F. Stockton, who had taken possession of California for the United States in 1846.

Susanville (Lassen County)

The town was named for Susan Roop, daughter of Isaac Roop, who settled in the region in 1853 and was recorder of the "Territory of Nataqua," formed in 1856.

Tahoe (Placer and El Dorado counties)

For a period of years, the lake was called "Lake Bigler", after California's third governor. "Tahoe" is an Indian word signifying "Big Water."

Tehachapi (Kern County)

This is the Indian name for a creek, and was recorded in 1853. Southern Pacific Railroad transferred the name from the old wagon route to the railroad pass.

Tehama (Tehama County)

For years the name has been construed to be of Indian origin, perhaps meaning "high water," perhaps referring to Sacramento River floods. Dr. Erwin G. Gudde, University of California, believed that Tehama is one of the few Aztec words in California, coming from the Mexican *"tejamanil"*.

Temecula (Riverside County and San Diego County)

An Indian rancheria was mentioned as *"Temeca" in 1797,* and as *"Temecula"* in 1820. The Indian word *"Temet"* means, "sun" in Luiseno Indian.

Thousand Palms (Riverside County)

The name reflects the fact that the largest group of Washingtonia palms found in California exists here.

Tiburon (Marin County)

The word means "shark", and *"Punta de Tiburon"* is mentioned in 1823.

Torrance (Los Angeles County)

The town was named after the owner of the land, Jared S. Torrance, in 1911.

Tracy (San Joaquin County)

Southern Pacific named it for one of its officials, Lathrop J. Tracy, in 1878.

Trona (San Bernardino County)

The town is named for the grayish-white mineral, a variety of potash, found in the lake.

Truckee (Placer and Nevada counties)

Both the river and the town were named for an Indian who piloted part of the Stevens party across the Sierra in 1844.

Tulare (Tulare County)

This is the Mexican word for cattails or places where tules grow, such as in the marshy sections of the state.

Tuolumne (Tuolumne County)

The river was named for Indians in the district. The word may be a corruption of the Indian word *"talmalamne"*, meaning stone houses or caves.

Turlock (Stanislaus County)

When John W. Mitchell, owner of the property for the railroad station, declined to have his name applied to it, the station was named after Turlough, a county in Mayo, Ireland.

Ukiah (Mendocino County)

The name was first recorded as "Yokaya" in 1845. It has been spelled Ukiah since 1856 when the town was founded. It comes from the Indian Yokaia, *"yo"* (South) and *"Ka-ia"* (valley).

Vacaville (Solano County)

It is not named after the Spanish word for cow (*vaca*) as many think, but after the Manual Vaca family that came from New Mexico in 1841 and settled in the district.

Vallejo (Solano County)

The town was named after Gen. Mariano Guadalupe Vallejo, of Sonoma. He was prominent in public affairs of California.

Vasquez Rocks (Los Angeles County)

One of California's most notorious bandits, Tiburcio Vasquez, had a hideout there in the 1870's.

Ventura (Ventura County)

The name is an abbreviation of San Buenaventura, the name given to the mission in 1782.

Victorville (San Bernardino County)

J.N. Victor was superintendent of the California Southern Pacific Railroad. The town was named for him.

Visalia (Tulare County)

The name was formed from that of Nathaniel Vise, a bear hunter and the reputed founder of Visalia, and that of his wife, Salia Matilda.

Watsonville (Santa Cruz County)

The post office was established in 1854 and named for Judge John H. Watson, owner of the land.

Woodland (Yolo County)

The wife of Major F.S. Freeman, who had bought the store of Henry Wyckoff while it was a small trading post, named it for the abundance of fine oak trees in the area.

Yuba

John Sutter applied the name to the river in 1839 or 1840. The name is after the Maidu Indian village opposite the mouth of the river.

About the Author

Alton Pryor has been a writer for magazines, newspapers, and wire services. He worked for United Press International in their Sacramento Bureau, handling both printed press as well as radio news.

He then journeyed to Salinas, where he worked for the Salinas Californian daily newspaper for five years.

In 1963, he joined California Farmer magazine where he worked as a field editor for 27 years. When that magazine was sold, the new owners forced him into retirement, which did not suit him at all.

He then turned to writing books. Alton Pryor is now (with this book) the author of seven books (see page 5). He is a graduate of California State Polytechnic University, San Luis Obispo, where he earned a Bachelor of Science degree in journalism.

Order Form

Stagecoach Publishing
5360 Campcreek Loop
Roseville, Ca. 95747-8009
(916) 771-8166
Fax: (916) 784-7466

Please send

____copies "Little Known Tales in California History"--$11.95
____copies "Classic Tales in California History"--$11.95
____copies "Outlaws and Gunslingers."--$11.95
____copies "California's Hidden Gold"--$11.95
____copies "Those Wild and Lusty Gold Camps"--$9.95
____copies "Historic California"--$9.95
____copies "Jonathan's Red Apple Tree"--$3.95

Name:_____

Address:_____

City:_____State:_____Zip:_____

Telephone: (___)_____

Shipping and handling: $3.00 for first book, and $1.00 each additional book.

Signature_____

Address_____

_____

_____

Telephone: _____